News for every
day of the year

Compiled by Hugh Morrison

Montpelier Publishing
London

Image credits: Loco Steve, Bert Verhoef, Teach Aids.org, John Shepherd, Eduard Marmet, Adam Smith, Egon Steiner, German Federal Archives, Greg Gjervingen, Dutch National Archives, Stevan Kragujevi, Steve Fitzgerald, Revista Gente, Brian Minkoff, Oliver F. Atkins, Georges Biard, Adam Bielawski, Syd Kat, Glotzer Management Company, Gordon Correll, Angela George, Paul C. Babin, Jim Summaria, Beeld and Geluid Wiki, Avda Photo.de, Vatican City, David Shankbone, Larry Rogers, Cezary Piwowarski, Bert Verhoeff/Anefo, Aldo Bidini, Sol Mednick, Adrian Pingstone, Oren Rozen, Land Rover MENA, Helge Overas, Roger Pic, Bob Moore, Emperor Ernie, Sergei Arssnyev, Diana Davis, Rob Dicaterino, Derek Redmond, Paul Campbell, Joost Evers/Enefo.

ISBN-13: 978-1725649569
ISBN-10: 172564956X

Published by Montpelier Publishing, London.
Printed and distributed by Amazon Createspace.

Events of
1969

Buzz Aldrin walks on the Moon

January 1969

Wednesday 1: Diminutive actor Verne Troyer born, best known as 'Mini Me' from the *Austin Powers* films. (Died 2018)

Thursday 2: Australian media baron Rupert Murdoch beats fellow tycoon Robert Maxwell in a bid to purchase the largest selling British Sunday newspaper, the *News of the World*.

Friday 3: Champion Formula One racing car driver Michael Schumacher born in Hurth, West Germany.

Saturday 4: Fighting breaks out during a civil rights march organised by the left-wing Peoples' Democracy group in Londonderry, Northern Ireland.

Sunday 5: 50 people killed as an Afghan airlines flight crashes into a house on its approach to Gatwick Airport, London.

Verne Troyer

Michael Schumacher

January 1969

Monday 6: Richard Nixon is elected President of the United States, defeating Democrat candidate Hubert Humphrey.

Tuesday 7: The trial begins of Sirhan Sirhan, the assassin of presidential candidate Robert F. Kennedy. The trial lasts 15 weeks and Sirhan is sentenced to death, later commuted to life imprisonment.

President Nixon

Wednesday 8: 23 people die in grass fires near Melbourne, Australia.

Thursday 9: A report commissioned by the United States Airforce finds no evidence of the existence of UFOs.

Friday 10: Long running US magazine *The Saturday Evening Post,* famous for its covers by Norman Rockwell, announces it will close in February.

Saturday 11: Sweden becomes the first country to grant formal diplomatic recognition to the Communist Republic of North Vietnam.

Sunday 12: The first Led Zeppelin album, *Led Zeppelin*, is released in the USA.

Sirhan Sirhan, Robert F. Kennedy's assassin

January 1969

Monday 13: 15 drown but 30 survive as a Scandinavian Airlines flight crashes in Santa Monica Bay off the coast of California.

Tuesday 14: The Soviet Union launches the Soyuz 4 rocket, the first Soviet space mission to be televised the same day.

Wednesday 15: The Soviet Union launches the Soyuz 5 rocket, which docks with Soyuz 4 the next day and collects its occupants.

Thursday 16: Student Jan Palach sets himself on fire in Prague, Czechoslovakia, in protest at the country's invasion by the Soviet Union.

Friday 17: The cosmonauts of the Soyuz missions return to earth in Soyuz 5.

Saturday 18: Preparations begin for the Paris Peace Talks to end the war in Vietnam.

Sunday 19: A United Airlines flight crashes into the Pacific Ocean near Los Angeles killing all 38 people on board.

Soyuz 5, which docked with Soyuz 4 on 16 January.

January 1969

Monday 20: Richard Nixon is sworn in as the 37th President of the United States.

Tuesday 21: The trial opens of Jim Garrison, suspected of involvement in the assassination of President John F Kennedy. He is found not guilty.

Nuclear submarine *NR-1*

Wednesday 22: Assassination attempt on Russian premier Leonid Brezhnev, by Viktor Ilyin, during a motorcade for the Soyuz cosmonauts.

Thursday 23: A tornado kills 29 people as it passes through the town of Hazlehurst, Mississippi, USA.

Friday 24: Spain's President Franco declares a three month state of emergency and suspension of civil rights following violent uprisings.

Saturday 25: *NR-1,* the smallest nuclear submarine ever built (147ft/45m) is launched at Groton, Connecticut, USA.

Sunday 26: Elvis Presley *(left)* begins recording his comeback sessions for the album *From Elvis in Memphis.*

January/February 1969

Monday 27: Controversial clergyman and Unionist leader the Reverend Ian Paisley is jailed for three months for illegal assembly in Northern Ireland.

Tuesday 28: The largest oil spill in US history to this date, approx 90,000 barrels, takes place off the coast of Santa Barbara, California.

DON'T WORRY — BE HAPPY.

MEHER BABA

Wednesday 29: 500 students take control of part of Sir George Williams University, Montreal, in protest at alleged racial discrimination. The protest ends on 11 February following a fire causing one million dollars of damage.

Thursday 30: The Beatles give their final public performance, on the rooftop of Apple Corps studios in Savile Row, London.

Friday 31: Indian mystic Meher Baba, who popularised the phrase 'Don't Worry, Be Happy', dies aged 74.

Saturday 1: President Nixon instructs national security adviser Henry Kissinger to begin secret negotiations with China.

Sunday 2: British-born actor Boris Karloff (William Henry Pratt), famous for playing Frankenstein's monster *(left)*, dies aged 81.

February 1969

Monday 3: In Cairo, Yasser Arafat *(right)* is elected as chairman of the Palestine Liberation Organization (PLO).

Tuesday 4: An express train is derailed between Trichinopoly and Madras, India, killing 25 people.

Wednesday 5: António de Oliveira Salazar, Prime Minister of Portugal since 1932, is released from hospital following a brain haemorrhage in 1968.

The Boeing 747 Jumbo Jet

Thursday 6: Residents of Anguilla vote for independence from the United Kingdom. British troops regain control on 19 March.

Friday 7: The highest wind speed in British history, 136 mph, is recorded at Kirkwall, Orkney.

Saturday 8: 4,400lb/2000kg of stones fall on and around the village of Pueblito de Allende, Mexico, following the explosion of the Allende Meteorite.

Sunday 9: The first test flight of the world's largest commercial airliner, the Boeing 747 Jumbo Jet, takes place at Everett, Washington, USA.

February 1969

Monday 10: Thailand holds its first democratic elections since a coup in 1958.

Tuesday 11: Actress Jennifer Aniston, (Rachel in *Friends*) born in Sherman Oaks, California.

Wednesday 12: The Barre Plan for the six Common Market (now EU) nations to co-ordinate economic and monetary policies is presented.

Thursday 13: 27 people are injured at the Canadian Stock Exchange in Montreal as Quebec nationalists set off time bombs.

Amitabh Bachchan

Friday 14: Pope Paul VI removes several saint's days from the church calendar, including St Valentine.

Saturday 15: Bollywood star Amitabh Bachchan signs his first film contract, for *Saat Hindustani.*

Sunday 16: A group of yachtsmen including four Americans and two Britons are arrested on suspicion of espionage in Chinese waters after being blown off course. They are held captive for seven weeks.

***Friends* star Jennifer Aniston, born on 11 February**

February 1969

Monday 17: Aquanaut Berry L Cannon dies while trying to repair the SEALAB III underwater research station off the coast of California. Following this the SEALAB programme is discontinued.

Tuesday 18: 8 people are killed and 11 injured after a train carrying tanks of ammonia gas crashes at Crete, Nebraska.

Wednesday 19: The USSR's unmanned Lunokhod moon rocket crashes shortly after take-off.

Thursday 20: US President Richard Nixon proposes, unsuccessfully, the abolition of the Electoral College voting system in the USA.

Friday 21: A second rocket disaster in two days occurs as the Soviet N1 moon rocket crashes shortly after liftoff.

Saturday 22: North Vietnam and Viet Cong forces attack South Vietnam in the final stage of the Tet Offensive.

Sunday 23: Following Communist attacks, President Nixon orders the bombing of Viet Cong guerrilla bases in neighbouring Cambodia.

Artist's impression of underwater research station SEALAB III

February/March 1969

Monday 24: The American *Mariner 6* probe is launched from Cape Kennedy, Florida, on its mission to Mars.

Tuesday 25: President Nixon announces the unilateral discontinuation of the US biological weapons programme.

Wednesday 26: The Prime Minister of Israel, Levi Eshkol, dies of a heart attack in Jerusalem. Arab guerillas claim it is the result of their rocket attack on his residence two days earlier.

Thursday 27: Silent film star John Boles, who played Victor Moritz in *Frankenstein* (1931) dies aged 73.

Friday 28: Sirhan Sirhan, on trial for the murder of Robert F Kennedy, changes his plea from innocent to guilty and asks to be executed.

Saturday 1: Doors frontman Jim Morrison *(above)* is accused of indecent exposure on stage in Miami, Florida and is later arrested. He is posthumously pardoned in 2010.

Sunday 2: The Anglo-French supersonic jet liner *Concorde (right)* makes its first test flight at Toulouse, France.

March 1969

Monday 3: NASA launches Apollo 9, which orbits the earth for ten days to test the lunar landing module.

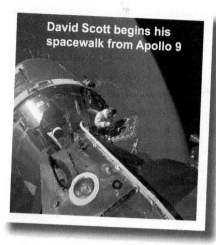
David Scott begins his spacewalk from Apollo 9

Tuesday 4: Notorious London gangsters the Kray Twins are found guilty of murder at the Old Bailey.

Wednesday 5: Joe Orton's play *What the Butler Saw* premieres in London.

Thursday 6: Apollo 9 astronauts undertake an hour-long 'space walk'.

Friday 7: Golda Meir elected as Israel's first female Prime Minister, following the sudden death of Levi Eshkol.

Saturday 8: McDonald's founder and CEO Ray Kroc (66) marries Joan Mansfield (40).

Sunday 9: Chief of staff of the Egyptian armed forces, General Abdul Munim Riad, is killed in a border skirmish with Israeli troops.

Golda Meir, Israel's first woman Prime Minister

March 1969

Monday 10: In Memphis, Tennessee, James Earl Ray pleads guilty to assassinating Martin Luther King Jr (he later makes a retraction).

Tuesday 11: Science fiction author John Wyndham, author of *The Day of the Triffids* and *The Midwich Cuckoos*, dies in Hampshire, England, aged 65.

Wednesday 12: Paul McCartney (26) marries Linda Eastman (27) in a civil ceremony at Marylebone Register Office, London.

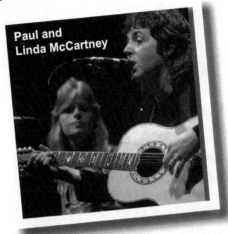

Paul and Linda McCartney

Thursday 13: Apollo 9 returns safely to Earth after successful testing of the lunar module.

Friday 14: West Indies cricketer Seymour Nurse retires after a score of 258 against New Zealand, the highest ever Test score for a cricketer in his final innings.

Saturday 15: Violent clashes take place between Russian and Chinese troops on Damansky Island on the Sino-Soviet border.

James Earl Ray

Sunday 16: 84 passengers and 71 people on the ground are killed as a DC-9 airliner en route for Miami crashes in Maracaibo, Venezuela.

March 1969

Monday 17: All eight crew of the Longhope lifeboat perish in severe storms at Pentland Firth, Orkney, Scotland.

Tuesday 18:
Operation Breakfast, the covert bombing of Viet Cong forces in Cambodia by the USAF, begins.

Wednesday 19:
British troops land in Anguilla, ending the country's unrecognised independence from the UK.

Yoko Ono and John Lennon

The 1263 ft/385m Emley Moor TV mast collapses in Yorkshire, England; nobody is injured but TV broadcasts are seriously disrupted.

Thursday 20: John Lennon and Yoko Ono are married in the British colony of Gibraltar. Their honeymoon is spent in Amsterdam where they undertake their 'bed-in' protest against the war in Vietnam.

Friday 21: Underground nuclear bomb tests take place in Nevada as part of Operation Bowline.

Saturday 22: Broadway flop *Come Summer* closes in New York after just seven performances. Despite this, lead actor David Cryer wins the 1970 Theater World Award for his performance in the show.

Sunday 23: Following Jim Morrison's arrest for exposure in the city, Miami teenagers stage a 'Rally for Decency'.

March 1969

Monday 24: John Lennon and Yoko Ono meet artist Salvador Dali in Paris.

Tuesday 25: Agha Muhammed Yahya Khan becomes the third President of Pakistan.

Wednesday 26: Soviet weather satellite *Meteor 1* is launched.

Thursday 27: NASA's probe *Mariner 7* is launched on a flyby mission to Mars.

Friday 28: Former US president and military commander Dwight D. Eisenhower ('Ike') dies aged 78.

Lulu

Saturday 29: In Madrid, Great Britain is joint winner of the Eurovision Song Contest with *Boom Bang-a-Bang* by Lulu.

Sunday 30: Widespread blackouts in Ulster following the explosion of a Loyalist bomb at Castlereagh power station.

Dwight D. Eisenhower

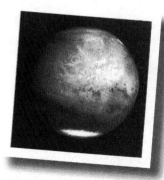

Mars photo by *Mariner 7*

March/April 1969

Monday 31: 153 coal miners killed in the Barroteran disaster in Mexico.

Tuesday 1: The Hawker Siddeley Harrier (vertical takeoff 'jump jet') enters service with the Royal Air Force. Able to take off and land in extremely limited spaces, it soon becomes a popular aircraft with many air forces including the USAF. It remains in service with the RAF until 2006.

Harrier in service with the USAF

Wednesday 2: Spanish-American singer and actor Fortunio Bonanova dies aged 74.

Thursday 3: The US government announces it will begin to reduce American involvement in Vietnam with a policy of 'Vietnamization' of the war effort.

Friday 4: Surgeon Denton Cooley implants the first temporary artificial heart, in Houston, Texas. The recipient, Mr Haskell Carp, survives for 65 hours.

Saturday 5: Large anti-Vietnam war demonstrations occur in several US cities.

Sunday 6 (Easter Sunday): The British Trans-Arctic Expedition, led by Wally Herbert, reaches the North Pole on foot.

April 1969

Monday 7: The US Supreme Court strikes down several state laws prohibiting possession of obscene publications.

Tuesday 8: American composer Arthur Walter Kramer, editor of *Musical America* magazine, dies aged 78.

Wednesday 9: The Harvard University administration building is seized by student demonstrators.

Harley J. Earl

Thursday 10: US automotive engineer Harley J. Earl, pioneer of the first 'tailfin' cars, dies aged 75.

Friday 11: Welsh singer Cerys Matthews of Catatonia born.

Saturday 12: Charlotta Bass, civil rights activist and editor of the *California Eagle,* dies aged 95. She is thought to be the first black woman to own and operate a newspaper in the USA.

Sunday 13: The final tram service ends in Brisbane, Australia, after 84 years of operation.

Cerys Matthews

April 1969

Monday 14: Katharine Hepburn and Barbra Streisand win the first ever tie for Best Actress at the 41st Academy Awards.

Tuesday 15: A US Navy Lockheed EC-121 aircraft is shot down by North Korean fighters over the sea of Japan with the loss of all crew.

Katherine Hepburn

Alexander Dubček

Wednesday 16: Milwaukee Brewers infielder Fernando Vina born in Sacramento, California.

Thursday 17: Alexander Dubček resigns as first secretary of Czechoslovakia's Communist Party in response to the Soviet invasion the previous year.

Friday 18: Princess Sayako of Japan, daughter of the present Emperor Akihito, born.

Saturday 19: Serious rioting in Londonderry following a civil rights march.

Sunday 20: British troops arrive in Northern Ireland to assist the civil powers in maintaining order. It becomes known as 'Operation Banner', the longest operation in British military history, lasting until July 2007.

April 1969

Monday 21: The British government announces that troops will be used to guard key public installations in Northern Ireland.

Tuesday 22: British sailor Robin Knox-Johnston becomes the first man to sail solo non-stop around the world, in 312 days.

Wednesday 23: Universal adult suffrage in local elections is introduced in Northern Ireland following civil rights protests.

Austin Maxi

Thursday 24: The recently formed British Leyland motor group in the UK launches its first model, the Austin Maxi. The car uses the space-saving design of the Mini scaled up to family car size.

Friday 25: The BBC airs the final episode of its long running serial *Mrs Dale's Diary*, first broadcast in 1948.

Saturday 26: Morihei Ueshiba, the founder of the Japanese martial art of Aikido, dies aged 85.

Sunday 27: Ballerina and *Strictly Come Dancing* judge Darcey Bussell *(right)* born.

April/May 1969

Monday 28: Charles de Gaulle steps down as President of France after defeat in the French constitutional election.

Tuesday 29: Actor Paul Adelstein (*Prison Break, Memoirs of a Geisha*) born in Chicago, Illinois.

Wednesday 30: Norway's Turi Widerøe becomes the first female pilot to fly for a major commercial airline.

Charles de Gaulle

Thursday 1: James Chichester-Clark becomes Prime Minister of Northern Ireland.

Friday 2: The *Queen Elizabeth II* (QE2) cruise liner leaves on its maiden voyage to New York.

Saturday 3: Zakir Husain, third President of India (1967-1969) dies aged 72.

Sunday 4: Writer Osbert Sitwell dies in Italy aged 76.

The QE2

May 1969

Monday 5: Normal Mailer is awarded the Pulitzer Prize for his political book *Armies of the Night.*

Tuesday 6: The government of Northern Ireland announces an amnesty for all offences associated with demonstrations since 5 October 1958, resulting in the release of the Reverend Ian Paisley, imprisoned for illegal assembly.

Wednesday 7: Six people are killed and 21 injured when a London to Aberdeen express train derails at Morpeth, Northumberland.

Thursday 8: Pope Paul VI continues his reforms of the Roman Catholic Church with the publication of S*acra Ritum Congregation.*

Friday 9: Carlos Lamarca begins communist guerilla action against the military dictatorship of Brazil in Sao Paulo.

Saturday 10: The Battle of Dong Ap Bia, known as 'Hamburger Hill' begins in Vietnam.

Sunday 11: The first script writing session of the BBC's 'Monty Python' comedy team takes place.

Wounded US troops evacuated from 'Hamburger Hill'

May 1969

Monday 12: Wing Commander Ken Wallis sets the world autogyro speed record of 111.2 mph (179 kph). Wallis designed the *Little Nellie* autogyro featured in the James Bond film *You Only Live Twice* (1967).

Tuesday 13: At least 196 people are killed as fighting breaks out between Malay and Chinese populations in Kuala Lumpur, Malaysia.

Wednesday 14: The Chevrolet Corvair, the only mass market American car to use a rear mounted, air cooled engine, ceases production.

Chevrolet Corvair

Thursday 15: An American teenager known only as 'Robert R' dies of a mysterious illness in St Louis, Missouri. In 1984 he is identified as the first case of HIV/AIDS in the USA.

Friday 16: The Soviet *Venera 5* space probe begins to orbit the planet Venus.

Saturday 17: *Venera 5's* auxiliary probe *Venera 6* begins its descent onto Venus, but is eventually crushed by atmospheric pressure.

Sunday 18: The Apollo 10 space mission, the 'full dress rehearsal' for the moon landings, is launched.

May 1969

Monday 19: Jazz saxophonist and composer Coleman Hawkins dies aged 64.

Tuesday 20: After brutal fighting, US troops in Vietnam capture Hill 937, 'Hamburger Hill'.

Wednesday 21: Sirhan Sirhan, the assassin of Robert F. Kennedy, is sentenced to death (later commuted to life imprisonment).

Thursday 22: Apollo 10's lunar module flies to within ten miles of the moon's surface.

Coleman Hawkins

Friday 23: The Who's fourth studio album, *Tommy*, is released; it is a 'rock opera' telling the story of Tommy, a deaf, dumb and blind boy.

Saturday 24: The Beatles' single *Get Back* hits number one in the US charts, where it stays for five weeks.

Sunday 25: The film *Midnight Cowboy* starring Dustin Hoffmann and Jon Voight is released in the USA.

Apollo I0 orbits the lunar surface

May/June 1969

Monday 26: The *Apollo 10* astronauts return to earth after successfully testing components for moon landing.

Tuesday 27: Construction begins on Walt Disney World near Orlando, Florida.

Wednesday 28: Milan beats Ajax 4-1 at the 13th European Cup Final in Madrid.

Thursday 29: Civil uprising against military rule takes place in Cordoba, Argentina.

Friday 30: Australia's Derek Clayton sets a world record marathon time of 2.08: 33.6 at Antwerp, Belgium.

Saturday 31: John Lennon and Yoko Ono record the song *Give Peace a Chance.*

Sunday 1: Tobacco advertising is banned on Canadian TV and radio.

Uprising in Cordoba, Argentina

June 1969

Monday 2: Murle Lindstrom wins the LPGA O'Sullivan Ladies' Golf Open.

Tuesday 3: 74 sailors killed as Royal Australian Navy carrier HMAS *Melbourne* accidentally collides with US Navy destroyer USS *Frank E Evans* on manoeuvres in the South China Sea.

Nixon meets Van Thieu at Midway Island

Wednesday 4: Armando Socarras Ramírez, 17, of Cuba, survives a 22 hour flight to Madrid inside the undercarriage of a Douglas DC-8 jet airliner. His companion, Jorge Perez Blacno, 16, does not survive the journey.

Thursday 5: The International Communist Conference begins in Moscow.

Friday 6: An outdoor church service takes place at Arlington National Cemetery, Virginia, to mark the first anniversary of the assassination of Robert F. Kennedy.

Saturday 7: *The Johnny Cash Show* debuts on ABC-TV in the USA.

Sunday 8: US President Richard Nixon and South Vietnamese President Nguyen Van Thieu meet at Midway Island in the Pacific. Nixon announces the withdrawal of 25,000 US troops from Vietnam by September.

June 1969

Monday 9: Brian Jones leaves the Rolling Stones due to drug addiction problems.

Brian Jones

Tuesday 10: British film actor Frank Lawton (*David Copperfield, Went The Day Well?*) dies aged 64.

Wednesday 11: The Beatles song *The Ballad of John and Yoko* hits number one in the UK charts.

Thursday 12: Brazil defeats England 2-1 during the end of season South American soccer tour.

Friday 13: Mick Taylor replaces Brian Jones in the Rolling Stones.

Saturday 14: John Lennon and Yoko Ono appear on the *David Frost Show* on British TV.

Sunday 15: Rapper 'Ice Cube' born.

Ice Cube

Mick Taylor

June 1969

Monday 16: Field Marshal Harold Alexander, 1st Earl Alexander of Tunis and 17th Governor General of Canada, dies aged 77.

Tuesday 17: The musical *Oh! Calcutta!* performed by an almost entirely nude cast, opens on Broadway.

Wednesday 18: *The Wild Bunch* directed by Sam Peckinpah and starring William Holden and Ernest Borgnine is released in cinemas.

Georges Pompidou

Thursday 19: The US 47th Infantry engages the Viet Cong in a bitter 23 hour battle in Long An Province, Vietnam.

Friday 20: Georges Pompidou is elected President of France.

Saturday 21: Approximately 600 communist troops storm a US base near Tay Ninh in Vietnam. Americans lose ten soldiers in the two day battle.

Sunday 22: Actress Judy Garland famous for her role as Dorothy in *The Wizard of Oz,* dies of a drug overdose in London, aged 47.

Judy Garland

June 1969

Monday 23: Warren E. Burger is sworn in as Chief Justice of the United States, replacing Earl Warren.

Tuesday 24: The United Kingdom and Rhodesia sever diplomatic ties following Rhodesia's decision to become a republic.

Wednesday 25: Pancho Gonzalez beats Charles Pasarell in a 5 hour 12 minute tennis match, the longest in the game's history up to that date.

The Stonewall Inn

Thursday 26: English musician Colin Greenwood (Radiohead) born in Oxford, England.

Friday 27: 50,000 people attend the Denver Pop Festival. Predating the Woodstock festival, it was one of the first large outdoor pop music gatherings.

Saturday 28: Police raid the Stonewall Inn gay bar in Greenwich Village, New York, resulting in three days of rioting.

Sunday 29: The first Jewish religious service to be held in the grounds of the White House in Washington takes place.

Warren E. Burger

June/July 1969

Monday 30: The Spanish colony of Ifni is ceded to Morocco.

Tuesday 1: Charles, Prince of Wales, is invested with his title at Caernarfon Castle, Wales.

Wednesday 2: Ireland defeats the West Indies cricket team, bowling them out for 25. It is the last time Ireland defeats a touring side until 2003.

Prince Charles Investitute medal, 1969

Thursday 3: Brian Jones, late of the Rolling Stones, drowns in his swimming pool in Sussex, England.

Friday 4: 140,000 attend the Atlanta Pop Festival featuring Led Zeppelin and Janis Joplin.

Saturday 5: The Rolling Stones play a free concert in London's Hyde Park.

Sunday 6: General Franco orders the closing of the border between Spain and the British colony of Gibraltar. It is not reopened until 1985.

Janis Joplin

July 1969

Monday 7: French is given equal status to English in the Canadian national government.

Tuesday 8: The phased withdrawal of US troops from Vietnam, completed in November 1972, begins as 800 men of the 9th Infantry Division are sent home.

Wednesday 9: Rear Admiral Raizo Tanaka, senior Japanese naval officer at the Battle of Guadalcanal in World War Two, dies aged 77.

Thursday 10: *Teignmouth Electron*, the boat belonging to *Sunday Times* round the world solo yacht competition entrant Donald Crowhurst, is found abandoned in the Atlantic. Crowhurst, later found to have cheated in the race, is missing, presumed drowned.

David Bowie

Friday 11: David Bowie's single *Space Oddity,* about the death of the astronaut 'Major Tom' is released in the UK.

Saturday 12: The Roman Catholic Church sets up an international Theological Commission to examine doctrine.

Sunday 13: Rod Stewart performs live with Led Zeppelin at the Singer Bowl, New York.

July 1969

Monday 14: The US $500, $1000, $5000 and $10,000 bills are withdrawn from circulation.

Tuesday 15: The United Nations security council issues its report on the Arab-Israeli ceasefire.

Wednesday 16: The Apollo 11 astronauts lift off towards the first moon landing.

Thursday 17: The crew of Apollo 11 make a live TV broadcast en route to the moon.

Friday 18: Senior Democrat senator Edward M. Kennedy crashes his car at Chappaquiddick Bridge, Massachusetts. His passenger, Mary Jo Kopechne, is drowned.

Saturday 19: Britain's John Fairfax becomes the first person to row solo across the Atlantic, after 180 days at sea in the 25' boat *Britannia*.

Sunday 20: Neil Armstrong takes his historic first steps on the moon at 10.56pm ET. It is watched on television by an estimated 500 million people worldwide.

Apollo 11 astronaut Buzz Aldrin walks on the moon

July 1969

Monday 21: The Soviet unmanned mission to the moon, intended to beat the Americans at bringing back lunar rock samples, ends in failure as the Luna 15 rocket crash lands during its descent to the moon.

Tuesday 22: Spanish dictator General Francisco Franco appoints Prince Juan Carlos, heir apparent to the throne of Spain, as his successor.

Wednesday 23: The BBC first broadcasts *Pot Black*, its long running snooker programme, with players including Ray Reardon and Fred Davis.

Thursday 24: The Apollo 11 astronauts return from the moon and are placed in isolation for several days.

Friday 25: US President Richard Nixon declares the Nixon Doctrine, beginning the process of American detachment from Vietnam.

Saturday 26: Sharon Sites Adams becomes the first woman to sail solo across the Pacific Ocean.

Sunday 27: South African cricketer Jonty Rhodes is born.

**Prince Juan
Carlos of Spain**

July/August 1969

Monday 28: Ramon Grau San Martin, President of Cuba, dies aged 87.

Tuesday 29: The Mariner 6 probe begins transmitting pictures of Mars.

Wednesday 30: US President Richard Nixon meets President Nguyen Van Thieu and US military commanders in Vietnam.

Thursday 31: The old halfpenny ($\frac{1}{2}$d), a coin with a history dating to the thirteenth century, ceases to be legal tender in the UK.

Pope Paul VI makes history as the first pope to visit Africa as he arrives in Entebbe, Uganda.

Old halfpenny

Friday 1: 110,000 attend the Atlantic City Pop Festival. Acts include Joni Mitchell, Jefferson Airplane and Creedence Clearwater Revival.

Saturday 2: US President Nixon makes a state visit to Romania.

Sunday 3: After a nine year public absence, Elvis Presley returns to live performance with a concert in Las Vegas, Nevada.

Pope Paul VI

August 1969

Monday 4: Secret peace negotiations begin in Paris between Henry Kissinger of the USA and Xuan Thuy of North Vietnam; no agreements are reached.

Tuesday 5: The Mariner 7 space probe, sister craft of Mariner 6 on NASA's Mars mission, makes its closest fly-by of the red planet (2189.7 miles/3524km).

Wednesday 6: Shinto and Christian ceremonies held in Hiroshima, Japan, to mark the twenty-fifth anniversary of the atomic bombing of the city.

Thursday 7: Scottish footballer and manager Paul Lambert born.

Sharon Tate

Friday 8: The Beatles are photographed on a zebra crossing on Abbey Road, London NW8, later used as the cover image for their album *Abbey Road*.

Saturday 9: Members of the Manson Family cult begin a two-day killing spree in Los Angeles, killing Sharon Tate, husband of film director Roman Polanski.

Sunday 10: The Manson Family murderers kill Los Angeles businessman Leno LaBianca and his wife, Rosemary. Police initially do not make any connection between this case and the killings of the previous day.

August 1969

Monday 11: Los Angeles Dodgers' Don Drysdale retires from professional baseball to begin his broadcasting career.

Tuesday 12: A three day sectarian riot known as the 'Battle of the Bogside' begins in Londonderry, Northern Ireland.

Don Drysdale

Wednesday 13: Border clashes occur between the Soviet Union and the People's Republic of China.

Thursday 14: Troops patrol Londonderry to maintain order in the first action of 'Operation Banner'.

Friday 15: The three-day Woodstock Festival is held in upstate New York.

Saturday 16: British troops are deployed in Belfast following serious public disorder.

Sunday 17: 248 people killed as Hurricane Camille, the second worst cyclone in US history, hits the Mississippi coast.

Hippies at the Woodstock Festival

August 1969

Monday 18: Mick Jagger is injured by a misfiring pistol while acting on the set of the film *Ned Kelly*.

Tuesday 19: Actor Matthew Perry (Chandler in *Friends*) born.

Wednesday 20: The Florissant Fossil Beds National Monument is established in Florissant, Colorado.

Thursday 21: Donald and Doris Fisher open the first Gap store on Ocean Avenue in San Francisco.

Matthew Perry

Friday 22: Gloria O. Smith of New York is crowned the second Miss Black America.

Saturday 23: Elvis Presley records his *Elvis at the International* live LP at the International Hotel, Las Vegas.

Sunday 24: Following severe fighting near Da Nang in Vietnam, exhausted men of the US Army's 196th Light Infantry Brigade stage a mutiny. No disciplinary action is taken but the incident is widely reported in the US media.

Mick Jagger

August 1969

Monday 25: Ho Chi Minh, president of North Vietnam, writes to US President Richard Nixon urging him to withdraw troops from South Vietnam; it is his last published document before his death.

Tuesday 26: Australian troops dedicate a battlefield memorial to comrades who died at Long Thanh, Vietnam, in 1966. 521 Australians in total gave their lives during the Vietnam war.

Soldiers of the Royal Australian Regiment arrive in Vietnam

Wednesday 27: A penumbral lunar eclipse takes place, visible across most of the Pacific Ocean and the western USA.

Thursday 28: Sheryl Sandberg, Chief Operating Officer of Facebook, born.

Friday 29: A Trans World Airlines flight from Rome to Tel Aviv is hijacked and diverted to Syria by members of the Popular Front for the Liberation of Palestine.

Saturday 30: 120,000 people attend the Texas International Pop Festival. Acts include Canned Heat and Janis Joplin.

Sunday 31: Bob Dylan and The Who are among the lineup at the Isle of Wight Festival, England.

September 1969

Ho Chi Minh

Colonel Gaddafi

Monday 1: A bloodless coup in Libya deposes King Idris and brings Colonel Muammar Gaddafi to power.

Tuesday 2: Ho Chi Minh, President of communist North Vietnam, dies aged 79.

Wednesday 3: The Michael Caine film *The Italian Job* is released in the USA.

Thursday 4: All seven crew are killed as a USAF B-52 bomber crashes on exercises near Limestone, Maine.

Friday 5: A court martial finds Lt William Calley of the US Army guilty of six counts of murder during the 'My Lai Massacre' of Vietnamese civilians in 1968.

Saturday 6: The hit musical *Cabaret* closes on Broadway after 1,165 performances.

Sunday 7: A documentary film about John Lennon and Yoko Ono's 'bed-in' protest in Amsterdam, *Mr and Mrs Lennon's Honeymoon*, premieres at the Edinburgh film festival.

September 1969

Monday 8: Major US game show host Bud Collyer *(right)* of *Beat the Clock* dies aged 61. He was also the voice of Superman in the 1940s radio adaptation of the cartoon.

Tuesday 9: 83 people killed as Allegheny Airlines flight 853 collides with a Piper light aircraft near Fairland, Indiana.

Wednesday 10: The Organisation of African Unity ratifies a convention to aid refugees throughout Africa.

Thursday 11: The USSR performs a nuclear test at Semipalitinsk in Kazakhstan.

Friday 12: US writer James Frey (*A Million Little Pieces*) born in Cleveland, Ohio.

Saturday 13: The first episode of *Scooby Doo* is broadcast on CBS TV in the USA.

Sunday 14: *Bad Moon Rising* by Creedence Clearwater Revival *(right)* hits the number one slot in the UK charts, where it stays for three weeks.

September 1969

Monday 15: The UN issues a resolution warning Israel to abide by the Geneva Convention in its response to unrest caused by an arson attack on the Al-Aqsa mosque in August.

Tuesday 16: Lunar astronaut Neil Armstrong addresses the US congress on the importance of continuing the 'space race'.

Mil Mi-24 attack helicopter

Wednesday 17: Boss nova star Astrud Gilberto records an album entitled, appropriately enough, *September 17 1969.*

Thursday 18: Far left terrorist Jane Alpert bombs the Federal Building in New York City.

Friday 19: The Soviet Mil Mi-24 'Hind' attack helicopter makes its first test flight.

Saturday 20: The last Warner Brothers 'Merrie Melodies' cinema cartoon, *Injun Trouble,* is released.

Sunday 21: Britain's Ron Hill wins the European Marathon in Athens with a time of 2:16:47.8.

Ron Hill

September 1969

Monday 22: Willie Mays of the San Francisco Giants becomes the first baseball player since Babe Ruth to hit 600 career home runs.

Tuesday 23: *Butch Cassidy and the Sundance Kid,* starring Paul Newman and Robert Redford is released in the USA.

Wednesday 24: The trial begins of the 'Chicago Eight' for incitement to riot during anti-Vietnam protests during the 1968 Democratic National Convention.

Willy Mays

Thursday 25: The international Organisation of the Islamic Conference is founded to represent Islam worldwide.

Friday 26: The Beatles release their eleventh studio album, *Abbey Road.* A huge commercial success, it is regarded by many as their best album.

Saturday 27: Nicolas Grunitzky, second President of Togo, dies aged 56.

Sunday 28: Social Democrats and Free Democrats form a coalition government following elections in West Germany.

Paul Newman

September/October 1969

Monday 29: Long running game show *Sale of the Century,* hosted by Jack Kelly (from western series *Maverick*) is first broadcast on NBC TV in the USA.

Tuesday 30: Elton John records the single *Border Song* at Maida Vale studios, London.

Gwen Stefani

Wednesday 1: The Anglo-French supersonic jet liner *Concorde* breaks the sound barrier for the first time.

Thursday 2: A 1.2 megaton thermonuclear device is tested at Amchitka Island, Alaska.

Friday 3: Singer Gwen Stefani of No Doubt (*It's My Life*) born in Fullerton, California.

Saturday 4: The last wooden cars on New York's Elevated line are retired; many are over fifty years old.

Sunday 5: *Monty Python's Flying Circus* is first broadcast on BBC TV.

Concorde

October 1969

Monday 6: Two helicopters of the 21st Special Operations Squadron are shot down near Muang Phine Laos, Vietnam. 54 USAF and native personnel are later saved in what is the most successful rescue effort of the Vietnam war.

Tuesday 7: The first episode of BBC cartoon series *Mary, Mungo and Midge*, narrated by Richard Baker, is broadcast.

Wednesday 8: Troops are brought in to maintain order as the radical 'Weathermen' group begins a series of violent anti government demonstrations, the 'Days of Rage' in Chicago.

Diana Ross and The Supremes

Thursday 9: Diana Ross and The Supremes release *Someday We'll Be Together*.

Friday 10: The Beatles' press officer, Derek Taylor, reassures the public that despite persistent rumours, Paul McCartney is not dead.

Saturday 11: The Soviets launch *Soyuz 6*, followed by *Soyuz 7* and *Soyuz 8* over the next two days, which carry out tests in orbit and return to earth on 16 October. During the mission, a record seven people are in earth orbit.

Sunday 12: Russo-French modernist painter Serge Poliakoff dies aged 69.

October 1969

Monday 13: A two-week unoffical miners' strike begins the UK, including all mines in Yorkshire.

Tuesday 14: Olof Palme becomes Prime Minister of Sweden.

Wednesday 15: Large demonstrations take place across the USA and Australia led by the Moratorium to End the War in Vietnam.

Olof Palme

Thursday 16: *Soyuz 6* returns to Earth, followed by *Soyuz 7* and 8 over the next two days.

Friday 17: Willard S. Boyle and George Smith invent the Charge Coupled Device (CCD), technology which later becomes an essential component of digital cameras.

Saturday 18: Rod Stewart and Ronnie Wood (later of the Rolling Stones) join Mod group The Small Faces; following the new lineup the band is renamed The Faces.

Sunday 19: Trey Parker, co-creator with Matt Stone of the *South Park* cartoon series, is born in Conifer, Colorado.

Rod Stewart

October 1969

Monday 20: In a campaign speech, future US President Gerald Ford denounces American 'radicals who want the Communists to take over South Vietnam'.

Tuesday 21: American 'beat generation' author Jack Kerouac (*On the Road*) dies from alcoholism in St Petersburg, Florida, aged 47.

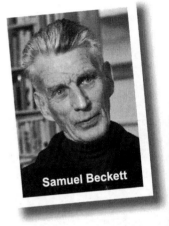

Samuel Beckett

Wednesday 22: In an interview with the BBC, Paul McCartney publicy denies rumours that he has been dead since 1966.

Thursday 23: Avant-garde Irish writer Samuel Beckett (*Waiting for Godot*) is announced as the winner of the Nobel Prize in Literature.

Ali McGraw

Friday 24: Actress Ali MacGraw (*Love Story*) marries film producer Robert Evans.

Saturday 25: John Gorton's Liberal coalition government is narrowly re-elected in Australia, defeating Gough Whitlam's Labor Party.

Sunday 26: The International Hockey Federation announces that the first hockey World Cup will be held in Pakistan in 1971.

October/November 1969

Monday 27: The British colony of St Vincent and the Grenadines is granted 'associate statehood' status; gaining full independence in 1979.

Tuesday 28: The Ministry of Agriculture, assisted by troops, culls all wildlife within a two mile radius of Camberley in Surrey, England, following an outbreak of rabies.

Wednesday 29: The first message ('Login') is sent in the USA across ARPANET, the forerunner of the internet.

Thursday 30: Jazz musician Pops Foster, who worked with King Oliver, Kid Ory and Sidney Bechet, dies aged 77.

Friday 31: The Walmart chain, founded in the USA in 1962, is incorporated as Wal-Mart Stores Inc.

Saturday 1: Aerospace contractors present plans to NASA for an 'Integrated Launch and Re-Entry Vehicle', later to become the Space Shuttle.

Early prototype of the Space Shuttle

Sunday 2: It is announced that the first 'Gay Pride' rally will take place in New York in June 1970.

November 1969

Monday 3: The Beatles' *Abbey Road* album hits number one in the US charts, remaining there for eleven weeks.

Tuesday 4: Actor Matthew McConaughey (*Dazed and Confused, The Wedding Planner*) born in Uvalde, Texas.

Wednesday 5: US President Richard Nixon announces that a US company will begin exploration for oil in the Gulf of Suez on behalf of Israel.

Thursday 6: Following a renewal of interest in the works of J.R.R. Tolkien (author of *The Lord of the Rings*), the Tolkien Society is founded in London.

Friday 7: Pink Floyd release their *Ummagumma* album.

Saturday 8: The first film directed by Steven Spielberg, the TV movie *Night Gallery* starring Joan Crawford, premieres on US television.

Sunday 9: A group of American Indians seizes the abandoned Alcatraz prison near San Francisco, in protest over civil liberties. They remain there for 19 weeks.

Grafitti from the Indian occupation of Alcatraz

November 1969

Monday 10: The first episode of children's TV series *Sesame Street* airs on the NET network in the USA.

Tuesday 11: The Beatles (with Billy Preston) release their single *Get Back.* It is the only Beatles single that credits another artist at their request, and the first of their singles to be released in stereo.

Wednesday 12: Dissident author Alexander Solzhenitsyn is expelled from the Soviet Writers' Union.

Alexander Solzhenitsyn

The crew of Apollo 12

Thursday 13: Dutch author/politician and critic of Islam, Ayaan Hirsi Ali, is born in Mogadishu, Somalia.

Friday 14: NASA launches Apollo 12, the second manned mission to the moon.

Saturday 15: Regular colour TV broadcasts begin in the UK on BBC1 and ITV.

Sunday 16: Children's puppet series *The Clangers* is first broadcast on the BBC.

November 1969

Monday 17: US and USSR representatives meet in Helsinki to begin the SALT 1 negotiations on disarmament.

Tuesday 18: British dance band leader Ted Heath dies aged 67.

Wednesday 19: Apollo 12 astronauts Charles Conrad and Alan Bean land in the Ocean of Storms on the moon.

Thursday 20: 87 people killed as Nigeria Airways Flight 825 crashes near Lagos, Nigeria; it is the first fatal crash involving a Vickers VC-10 airliner.

Friday 21: Following talks with Japanese Prime Minister Eisaku Satō, US President Richard Nixon agrees to return the island of Okinawa, under US occupation since 1945, to Japanese control by 1972.

Saturday 22: The Pact of San José, also known as the American Convention on Human Rights, is signed in Costa Rica, involving most Latin American countries.

Sunday 23: The crew of Apollo 12 hold a televised news conference, 108,000 miles from Earth, while returning from the moon.

Satō and Nixon discuss the future of Okinawa

November 1969

Monday 24: The crew of Apollo 12 return from the moon. En route, they photograph an eclipse of the sun by the earth.

Tuesday 25: John Lennon returns his MBE in protest at British involvement in the Nigerian (Biafran) civil war.

Wednesday 26: The Draft Lottery becomes law in the USA; selective military conscription for men born between 1944 and 1950 is based on birthdates drawn from a lottery.

John Lennon

Thursday 27: German Chancellor Willy Brandt writes to French President Georges Pompidou urging expansion of the Common Market (later the European Union).

Willy Brandt

Friday 28: A 22 year old graduate student, Betsy Ruth Aardsma, is stabbed to death in the library at Pennsylvania State University; her killer is never caught.

Saturday 29: The Beatles single *Come Together* hits number one on the US singles chart.

Sunday 30: The USSR performs a nuclear test at Semipalitinsk, Kazakhstan.

December 1969

Monday 1: The first Draft Lottery in the USA since the Second World War takes place to choose conscripts for Vietnam.

Tuesday 2: The Boeing 747 'jumbo jet' makes its first commercial passenger flight, from Seattle to New York City.

Wednesday 3: Owner and chairman of the New York Yankees, Harold Steinbrenner, born in Culver, Indiana.

Thursday 4: Political radicals Fred Hampton and Mark Clark of the Black Panther Party are shot dead by police in Chicago.

Friday 5: The Rolling Stones' album *Let it Bleed* is released.

Saturday 6: The Rolling Stones host the Altamont Free Concert in California. Marred by violence, including the killing of an audience member by security guards, it is considered by many to mark the end of 1960s idealism.

Sunday 7: Popular US Christmas annual cartoon special *Frosty the Snowman*, voiced by comedian Jimmy Durante, premieres on CBS TV.

Jimmy Durante, voice of 'Frosty the Snowman'

December 1969

Monday 8: A four hour shootout takes place between police and members of the Black Panther Party in southern California. Police use the heavily armed SWAT (Special Weapons and Tactics) team for the first time.

Jakob Dylan

Tuesday 9: Singer and songwriter Jakob Dylan, lead singer of the Wallflowers and son of Bob Dylan, is born in New York.

Wednesday 10: Italian conductor Franco Capuana dies while leading a performance of Rossini's *Mosè in Egitto* in Naples, aged 75.

Thursday 11: The Revolutionary Command Council of Libya brings the country's new constitution into effect.

Friday 12: 17 people are killed when a bomb explodes at the National Agrarian Bank in the Piazza Fontana, Milan, Italy, thought to be planted by right wing extremists.

Saturday 13: Pioneering black film producer and actor Spencer Williams (*The Amos 'n' Andy Show*) dies aged 76.

Sunday 14: 25 year old telephonist Diane Maxwell is murdered in Houston, Texas. Her killer, James Ray Davis, is not found until 2003 when he is convicted using DNA evidence.

December 1969

Monday 15: John Lennon and Yoko Ono's new group, the Plastic Ono Band, plays its first public performance at London's Lyceum Theatre.

Tuesday 16: The British parliament votes to permanently abolish the death penalty, suspended since 1965.

Wednesday 17: Ukelele player and singer Tiny Tim (*Tiptoe Through The Tulips*) marries Miss Vicki Budinger live on the *Johnny Carson Show.*

Thursday 18: The sixth James Bond film, *On Her Majesty's Secret Service*, starring George Lazenby and Diana Rigg, premieres in London.

Friday 19: TV presenter Richard Hammond (*Top Gear*) born in Solihull, West Midlands.

Saturday 20: *Leaving on a Jet Plane* written by John Denver and sung by Peter Paul and Mary reaches number one in the US charts, the group's only chart-topping hit.

Sunday 21: Diana Ross makes her final public appearance as a member of the Supremes on the Ed Sullivan Show, before beginning a solo career.

Peter Paul and Mary

December 1969

Monday 22: The National Environmental Policy Act (NEPA), known as the 'Magna Carta' of environmental laws is passed in the US.

Tuesday 23: The El Al Flight 432 hijackers are sentenced to 12 years imprisonment; Israel admits that undercover agents are used on flights to combat hijacks.

Wednesday 24: North Sea oil is discovered by Phillips Petroleum in Norwegian waters.

Thursday 25: Israeli forces sieze five missile boats from Amiot Shipyard in Cherbourg, France; they had been paid for but not delivered due to a French arms embargo.

Friday 26: 20 die as snowdrifts of up to 30 ft (9.1m) cover upstate New York and New England.

Saturday 27: Israeli troops complete 'Operation Rooster', capturing an Egyptian mobile radar station in the Sinai Peninsula and returning it to Israel via helicopter.

Sunday 28: Software engineer Linus Torvalds, developer of the Linux operating system, born in Helsinki, Finland.

Captured Egyptian mobile radar at the Israeli Air Force Museum

December 1969

Monday 29: BAFTA award winning actress Jennifer Ehle (*Pride and Prejudice*) born in North Carolina, USA.

Tuesday 30: Three unarmed police officers are shot (two fatally) following a bank robbery at Linwood, near Glasgow. The gang leader, former policeman Howard Wilson, is later sentenced to 32 years in prison.

Wednesday 31: *Pop Go the Sixties,* a colour TV retrospective of the decade's music, is shown on BBC TV, with numerous live acts including The Who, Adam Faith, The Kinks, Cliff Richard and the Shadows and Cilla Black.

**Clockwise from left:
Cilla Black, Adam
Faith, Cliff Richard**

BIRTHDAY NOTEBOOKS

FROM
MONTPELIER PUBLISHING

Handy 60-page ruled notebooks with a significant event of the year on each page.

A great alternative to a birthday card.
Available from Amazon.

Made in the
USA
Columbia, SC